SUSTAINING CONTRACTUAL BUSINESS:

An Exploration of the New Revised International Commercial Terms

Incoterms®2010

K.B. CHIKWAVA

Copyright © 2012 by K.B. Chikwava.

ISBN: Softcover   978-1-4771-0073-8
             Ebook   978-1-4771-0074-5

This book was printed in the United States of America.

To order additional copies of this book, contact:
Xlibris Corporation
0-800-644-6988
www.xlibrispublishing.co.uk
Orders@xlibrispublishing.co.uk

Contents

About the author . . .

Brian K Chikwava is an International Trade and Logistics Professional with extensive experience in International Trade, Freight Forwarding, Logistics and Supply Chain Management. He is a Senior Logistics Advisor to the South African parastatal and utility company, in its Supply Chain Operations Division within Group Commercial.

He has held senior positions at Combine Cargo and Allen Wack and Shepherd Freight in Zimbabwe and has worked for United Airlines and the logistics company, Transoceanic (now Agility) in the United Kingdom. While working for Transoceanic as a project coordinator, from his London base he successfully synchronised the logistics of the construction of one of the major petro-chemical plants in Damman, Saudi Arabia (the 'SHARQ Project,)

He is accredited by the International Chamber of Commerce (ICC) in Paris as a Master Class Incoterms® 2010[1] Trainer. He is also a certified facilitator; having trained thousands of people in South Africa, He has also conducted workshops at the University of Johannesburg and school of Shipping across the country. He is a qualified and certified European Master Logistician (EMLog) and is also affiliated to the Chartered Institute of Purchasing and Supply (CIPS) and the Institute of Commercial Management (ICM).

---

[1] 'Incoterms' is a registered trademark of the International Chamber of Commerce that is registered in several countries.

. . . and how to use the book

This book summarises the topics, concepts and issues pertaining to the use of Incoterms in contracts. It also provides guidelines for the course material, why it is important and how to apply theories and concepts. While—as a supplementary text to facilitate learning—it is not intended to replace textbooks or lectures, it should be read in parallel with the ICC Incoterms® 2010 handbook, where each topic is covered in detail. It should be seen as a framework in which to organise the subject-matter and to extract crucial points from the textbook and other learning material.

Note that the views expressed in this handbook are intended as general interpretative guidance only and not as authoritative opinion.

Introduction

The International Commercial Terms, popularly known as 'Incoterms,' were formulated in 1936 in order to facilitate global trade by providing clear definitions of each party's obligations in a contract of sale, thereby reducing the potential for legal complications. According to Emmanuel Jolive, General Counsel of the International Court of Arbitration:

> 'The Incoterms are a perfect example of an efficient standardization of an international business tool.'

Their day-to-day use in international sales contracts brings legal certainty to business transactions, while at the same time simplifying the drafting of international contracts.

They are primarily relevant to companies involved in buying and selling *goods* internationally as their normal business. It is important to note that Incoterms are not applicable when dealing with *services*—a common misconception among most international trade practitioners. However, a debate has arisen about whether Incoterms should be used when either importing or exporting electricity to or from another country

The rules are also beginning to be incorporated into many domestic sales contracts, as per the new revised Incoterms® 2010.

Many companies are currently concluding contracts with external suppliers that involve the buying and selling of goods internationally without the use of a stipulated or specified Incoterm. This has cost many of these companies millions in losses as a result of disputes that may arise out of their lack of understanding of these very important rules. It is therefore always advisable to incorporate a specific Incoterm clause in any contract of sale in order to avoid possible legal action that could eventually result in the loss of business or in litigation against a specific company.

This publication examines and assesses the importance of incorporating the Incoterms into the contracts that involve business-to-business transactions.

Furthermore, it explores some features introduced by the new set of revised Incoterms 2010 that came into effect on 1 January 2011.

The latest terms were revised by a drafting committee comprising representatives from seven countries who met nine times from mid-2008. The three drafts they produced were presented to ICC national committees for comment; their comments were reviewed and incorporated into a final text.

It is interesting to observe that, since its inception in 1923, the ICC International Court of Arbitration has received 14 000 cases resulting from misrepresentation or a basic lack of understanding of these terms. The need to revise Incoterms can be attributed to the ever-increasing number of cases received by the arbitration board and also as a response to developing technology and also increasing use of these terms globally.

This publication further clarifies some of the misconceptions that have been associated with these important terms and examines to what extent their usage sustains contractual business.

Historical background to Incoterms

Incoterms is an abbreviation for 'International Commercial Terms', a body of pre-defined commercial terms created by the ICC in 1936.

Since their promulgation as internationally recognised terms by the ICC in 1939, these rules have undergone eight revisions in an effort to keep pace with rapidly expanding global trade. The changes and revisions were also necessitated by increasing security risks (especially after the 11 September 2001 World Trade Centre bombing in the United States) as well as a response to developing technology and also to increasing worldwide use of these terms.

Although they were developed to deal with different types of transaction, each in a particular context, they are generally defined as a series of predefined commercial terms published by the ICC and widely used in international commercial transactions. Originally, a series of *three-letter trade terms* (written in English) related to common sales practices.

The first set of Incoterms remained in use for almost 20 years until a second set was published in 1953. Additional amendments and expansions followed in 1967, 1976, 1980, 1990 and 2000.

The eighth and current version of the Incoterms rules—Incoterms 2010—was published and came into effect on 1 January 2011, hence the need to understand these new revised terms and their correct interpretation.

Why were they developed?

Incoterms rules are accepted by governments, legal authorities and practitioners worldwide for the interpretation of the terms most commonly used in international trade.

They were developed for the following reasons:

1. They either reduce or remove altogether any uncertainty arising from different interpretations of such terms in different countries.
2. According to the ICC, the purpose of Incoterms is to provide a set of international rules for the interpretation of the most commonly used trade terms in foreign trade.
3. The Incoterms define the responsibilities of buyers and sellers for the delivery of goods under sales contracts.
4. The Incoterms rules are intended primarily to clearly communicate the tasks, costs and risks associated with the transportation and delivery of goods.
5. They were developed to facilitate global trade by providing clear definitions of each party's obligations, thus reducing the potential for legal implications.

Who should use Incoterms?

The role of an appropriate supply-chain strategy, combined with the choice of logistics providers and supply-chain technology, is becoming increasingly important to organisations that wish to gain and maintain a competitive advantage. The variety of businesses that exist today require certain companies and professionals to make use of Incoterms and choose appropriate terms for a particular situation to avoid a loss of business and even legal action.

The following professionals may find the terms useful in their day-to-day business:

1. Contract negotiators or traders.
2. Execution operatives in organisations that export goods.
3. Logistics operatives with transport or shipping companies or with freight forwarders.
4. Trade finance officers in banks.
5. Export/import consultants and advisors.
6. Professionals working in finance and risk departments.
7. In-house cargo insurance specialists with insurance companies.
8. Lawyers advising any of the above and international bankers.

For international buyers and sellers, it is imperative to understand how to use these rules properly in their sale and/or purchase contracts They should also learn how to choose the correct Incoterm, as doing so could affect their obligations and, ultimately, their bottom line.

After scanning the list of Incoterms, one can conclude that they are critical across many business sectors and therefore should be considered to be rules vital to adhere to in multidisciplinary areas of business.

Some categories of business that uses Incoterms include trading companies, especially exporters and importers; marine and multimodal transport firms; logistics companies, and financial services businesses that provide funding for trading companies.

Common misconceptions about Incoterms

It appears that a number of misconceptions about Incoterms are in circulation. They are fairly commonplace, but have the potential to be extremely costly in terms of contractual obligations.

For example, the terms of the new set of revised Incoterms 2010 stipulate which party to the sale contract has the obligation to make carriage or insurance arrangements, especially when the seller delivers the goods to the buyer. They also indicate which costs each party is responsible for.

It is, however, important to stress that the Incoterms are silent about the price to be paid or the method of payment—which, in one opinion, would be a totally different contract altogether (a contract of payment). In addition, the Incoterms do not deal with either the transfer of ownership of goods or the consequences of a breach of contract. These matters are (or should be) dealt with through express terms in the contract of sale for a given transaction or shipment or by the law governing that contract. The parties involved should be aware that mandatory law may override any aspect of the sale contract, including the chosen Incoterm rule.

Furthermore, it is also common practice that Incoterms are frequently misunderstood as applying to the *contract of carriage* rather than to the *contract of sale*. They are sometimes wrongly assumed to provide for all the duties that parties may wish to include in a contract of sale. For example, while it is essential for exporters and importers to consider the very practical relationship that can exist between the various contracts needed to perform an international sales transaction—where not only the contract of sale is required, but also contracts of carriage, insurance and financing—Incoterms relate to only one of these contracts, namely, the contract of sale.

It is therefore critical to all those involved in the conclusion and negotiation of contracts involving business-to-business transactions to understand fully the limitations of Incoterms and to have a complete understanding not only of how to apply them but also how to choose the appropriate Incoterm for a specific situation with a full understanding and appreciation that Incoterms do not form a comprehensive contract of sale.

It should, however, be further stressed that the Incoterms are not intended to replace such contract terms that are required in any event for a complete contract of sale, either by the incorporation of standard terms or by individually negotiated terms.

A good example would be when the method of payment is not given due consideration by the Incoterm. It would be essential to incorporate an agreed method of payment. Many large companies involved in international business transactions use different types of methods of payment in their contracts; for present purposes, they can be categorised as 'Payment Method 1' and 'Payment Method 2'.

An example of the use of the different payment methods

Payment Method 1

Where prices are quoted in a foreign currency—that is, payment in a foreign currency to a nominated foreign bank account is considered the standard payment method.

Payment Method 2

Payment of foreign currency into a local Client Foreign Currency (CFC) account. It is the responsibility of the *supplier* to open the required CFC account in accordance with particular Reserve Bank requirements, and to ensure that the CFC account remains valid for the period of the contract to enable payments to be made. However, it is important to note that, the use of Payment Method 1b is not permitted for the procurement of services.

Nevertheless, the parties' agreement to use a particular Incoterm would necessarily have implications for the other contracts. A good example would be the case where a seller, having agreed to a Cost and Freight (CFR)—or Cost, Insurance and Freight (CIF)—contract, cannot perform such a contract by any other mode of transport than carriage by sea, since under these terms they must present a bill of lading or other maritime document to the buyer, which is simply not possible if other modes of transport such as air or road are used. Furthermore, the document required under a documentary credit would necessarily depend upon the means of transport intended to be used.

Incoterms: rules for any mode or modes of transport

The new terms used in the revised Incoterms® 2010 Rules for Trade are:

EXW: **EX WORKS**
            (named place)
FCA: **FREE CARRIER**
            (named place)
FAS: **FREE ALONGSIDE SHIP**
            (named port of shipment)
FOB: **FREE ON BOARD**
            (named port of shipment
CFR: **COST AND FREIGHT**
            (named port of destination)
CIF: **COST, INSURANCE AND FREIGHT**
            (named port of destination)
CPT: **CARRIAGE PAID TO**
            (named place of destination)
CIP: **CARRIAGE AND INSURANCE PAID TO**
            (named place of destination)
DAT: **DELIVERED AT TERMINAL**
            (named terminal)
DAP: **DELIVERED AT PLACE**
            (named place of destination)
DDP: **DELIVERED DUTY PAID**
            (named place of destination)

Four groups of Incoterms

The Incoterms have been grouped or put together in four different groups: **E**, **F**, **C** and **D**.

Group E: This group stands for 'Ex' (from) and starts with minimum responsibility and obligation for the seller, and maximum responsibility and obligation for the buyer. Under this group, the seller is responsible only for making the goods available to the buyer at the agreed place, usually at the seller's premises, but it could be at some or other works, factory or warehouse. The seller does not load goods onto the collecting vehicle.

Group F: This group continues with 'free' of responsibility during the main carriage from the seller's point of view. In this case, however, the seller is called upon to deliver the goods to a carrier appointed by the buyer. Here the seller is not responsible for the main carriage, but only for some pre-shipment charges.

Group C: This group stands for 'cost' or 'carriage' and entails the seller being responsible for contracting and paying for the main carriage, but without assuming the risk of loss of or damage to the goods, or additional costs due to events occurring after shipment and despatch

Group D: Finally, Group D means delivery and rallies 'arrival' Incoterms where the seller is responsible for delivery of the goods to the country of destination, bearing all costs and risks required to deliver the goods to the country of destination. The two newly introduced Incoterms, DAT and DAP, fall under this category.

Particularly in the realm of freight forwarding practice, the Incoterms can be divided further into two categories:

'Freight Prepaid': This is where the seller pays the main carriage charges before the departure of a consignment. Therefore, the seller is responsible for the costs of the main carriage. This category rallies groups C and D.

'Freight collect': Under this arrangement, the main carriage charges are collected, or payable, at destination, which means the buyer is paying for them and groups E and F are involved.

The classification of the 11 new Incoterms rules

Group	Refers to any mode of transport	Refers to sea and inland waterway transport only
Group E—Departure The seller makes the goods available to the buyer at the seller's own premises.	**EXW-Ex Works** (maximum obligation to buyer)	
Group F—Main Carriage Unpaid The seller is called upon to deliver the goods to a carrier appointed by the buyer.	**FCA** (Free Carrier)	**FAS** (Free Alongside Ship) **FOB** (Free On Board)
Group C—Main Carriage Paid The seller has to contract for carriage but without assuming the risk of loss or damage to the goods or additional costs due to events occurring after the shipment and dispatch.	**CPT** (Carriage Paid To) **CIP** (Carriage and Insurance Paid To)	**CFR** (Cost and Freight) **CIF** (Cost, Insurance and Freight)

Group D—Arrival	DAT	
The seller has to bear all costs and risks required to deliver the goods to the country of destination	(Delivered At Terminal) **DAP** (Delivered At Place) **DDP—Deliver Duty Paid** (maximum obligation to seller)	

As shown on the classification table above, the first class includes the seven Incoterms rules that can be used irrespective of the mode of transport selected and irrespective of whether one or more than one mode is employed. EXW, FCA, CPT, CIP, DAT, DAP and DDP all belong to this category or class. It is important to understand that these can be used even when there is no maritime transport at all; more importantly, the rules in this category can be applied in cases where a ship is used for only part of the carriage

The second category of Incoterms rules, the point of delivery and the place to which the goods are carried to the buyer are both ports, hence the label 'sea and inland waterway' rules. The names of the rules that fall under this category are FAS, FOB, CFR and CIF.

Nevertheless, it is important to highlight that under FOB, CFR and CIF there is a requirement to place the goods on board the vessel, so the responsibility of the seller ends when the goods have been 'delivered' on board the vessel. This is a true reflection of modern commercial reality and avoids the rather dated image of the risk swinging to and fro across an imaginary perpendicular line.

Incoterms® 2010 and what they mean

1 **EXW—Ex Works:** the seller 'delivers' when he or she places the goods at the disposal of the buyer at the seller's premises or another named place (that is, one or other works, factory or warehouse). The goods will not have been cleared for export and not loaded onto any collecting vehicle.

Under Ex-Works the seller is not obliged to load the goods onto the buyer's collecting vehicle

Under Ex-Works the seller has no obligation to load the goods, even though they may be in a better position to do so.

2 **FCA—Free Carrier:** the seller delivers the goods, cleared for export, to the carrier nominated by the buyer at the named place. It should be noted that the chosen place of delivery has

23

an impact on the obligations of loading and unloading the goods at that place. If delivery occurs at the seller's premises, the seller is responsible for loading. If delivery occurs at any other place, the seller is not responsible for unloading.

3   **CPT—Carriage Paid To:** the seller delivers the goods to the carrier nominated by him or her but the seller must, in addition, pay the cost of carriage necessary to deliver the goods to the named destination.

4   **CIP—Carriage and Insurance Paid To:** the seller delivers the goods to the carrier nominated by them but the seller must in addition pay the cost of carriage necessary to deliver the goods to the named destination and also pay the necessary insurance. Here the seller is obliged to provide only minimum coverage in line with the Cargo Clause C that is, cover for loss or damage between the point of departure and the destination stipulated.

5   **DAT (*new*)—Delivered At Terminal:** the seller is considered to have delivered when the goods, once unloaded from the arriving means of transport, are placed at the disposal of the buyer at a named terminal at the named port or place of destination. Common practice has it that whenever someone hears the word 'Terminal', he or she will think of the airport or seaport. When dealing with Incoterms, however, it is important to note that the word 'Terminal' is defined differently. This is necessitated by the fact that new revised Incoterms 2010 can be used for domestic trade therefore the word 'Terminal' in this case includes any place, whether covered or not, such as a quay, warehouse, container yard or road, rail or air cargo terminal.

Under this term the seller must bear all costs and risks in bringing the goods to and unloading them at the terminal at the named port of destination. In addition to these obligations, the seller must also clear the goods for export under what is generally referred to as 'Export Clearances', where applicable. However, the seller has no obligation either to clear the goods for import or to pay any import duty or carry out any import customs formalities.

6   **DAP (*new*)—Delivered At Place:** the seller is considered to have delivered when the goods are placed at the disposal of

the buyer on the arriving means of transport ready for unloading at the named place of destination. The critical part of this new Incoterm is that all parties under what circumstances must clearly specify as clearly as possible the point within the agreed place of destination as the risks to that point are the account of the seller. In this regard, it is also very important to note that since the seller under DAP is responsible the procuring the contract of carriage he or she has to make sure that he or she procures the contracts of carriage that matches and conform precisely to the buyers choice.

7   **DDP—Delivered Duty Paid:** the seller delivers the goods to the buyer, cleared for import and not unloaded from any arriving means of transport at the named place of destination. Under DDP there is maximum obligation to the seller and, on the other hand, this option allows minimum obligation on the buyer. The only responsibility of the buyer under DDP is to offload at the delivery place. The author has always advised international trade practitioners as well as contracts managers not to use DDP, if the seller is unable to directly or indirectly obtain import clearances. Instead DAP is recommended under such circumstances. Any VAT or other taxes payable upon import are for the seller's account unless expressly agreed otherwise in the sales contract.

8   **FAS—Free Alongside Ship:** the seller is considered to have delivered when the goods are placed alongside the vessel at the named port of shipment. This means that the buyer has to bear all costs and risks of loss of or damage to the goods from that moment.

A question under this Incoterm would be: Can the seller select a point other than physically 'alongside the ship? Therefore it is essential that under FAS the buyer indicates a loading point at the named port of shipment and under article B7 must give the seller sufficient notice of the vessel's name, loading point and, where necessary, selected delivery time within the agreed period.

Further to this, in the event that the buyer fails to give these details, the seller may use his discretion to select a point that best suits his purposes; but, in any case, that point should be alongside the ship.

In the event that the buyer has given an indication of the loading point but later wishes to change these instructions, the seller is not obliged to cover the cost of transferring the goods to a new loading point, provided that the seller has acted in line with the buyer's first instruction.

9 **FOB—Free On Board:** the seller is considered to have delivered when the goods are placed on board the ship at the named port of shipment. However, it sounds as if, with the new revised Incoterms, most people will no longer use FOB/CFR/CIF for container-loaded goods. This is because, where goods in a container are sold FOB, the container (as we all know) is typically handed over by the seller at a container yard or warehouse, which is in practice the appropriate delivery point.

Given that under FOB, according to the ICC Incoterm®' 2010 book, the seller bears all the costs, risks of loss of and damage to the goods until they are delivered by being placed on board the vessel, it is critical and recommended that for all containerised goods, buyers must opt for Incoterms such as FCA, CPT or CIP in such situations or circumstances. These options for containerised goods are recommended because under these rules, the risk is typically transferred to the buyer when the seller hands the goods over to the carrier—usually earlier than when being placed on board. In practice, this literally means one cannot use the FOB Incoterm in the case of containerised goods as per the new revised Incoterms 2010 rules.

10 **CFR—Cost and Freight:** the seller is considered to have delivered when the goods are placed on board the ship in the port of shipment. The seller must, in addition, pay the cost of carriage necessary to bring the goods to the named destination. Although under this Incoterm the issue of insurance is silent, it is assumed that the buyer purchases his or her own insurance.

11 CIF—Cost Insurance and Freight: the seller is considered to have delivered when the goods are placed on board the ship in the port of shipment and also pays the necessary freight and insurance (CIF). It is important to note that contracts placed CIF relieve the buyer of the task of making insurance arrangements. However, the disadvantages are many: under CIF the supplier is obliged only to buy the cheapest insurance coverage subject to cargo clauses C, unless otherwise stated in the bidding document contract that the coverage must be subject to 'Institute Marine Cargo Clauses, A'. Further to this, another disadvantage is that every insurance contract is placed with a different company by someone acting on behalf of the buyer only, each time with varying terms and conditions on minimum amounts for survey reports, coverage, and agents to contact with different procedures for payment of claims. For each of these insurance companies, the consignees are just one of their many occasional clients. This can lead to difficulties and non-payment of claims, if all the conditions stipulated in the policy/ certificates are not met (documentation incomplete, late presentation of claim, etc.). For the consignees, it means no continuity or standardisation in procedure. Finally, it may result in higher premium for a lesser coverage. The buyer may instead take advantage of corporate system-wide long-term-agreements for insurance coverage,maintained by headquarters.

This is a summary and brief description of what Incoterms mean. However, readers are encouraged to supplement their understanding of these rules by consulting the relevant ICC publications: *Incoterms®️ 2010 Rules ICC*

Guide to Incoterms® 2010.

Incoterms (2010 flow chart)

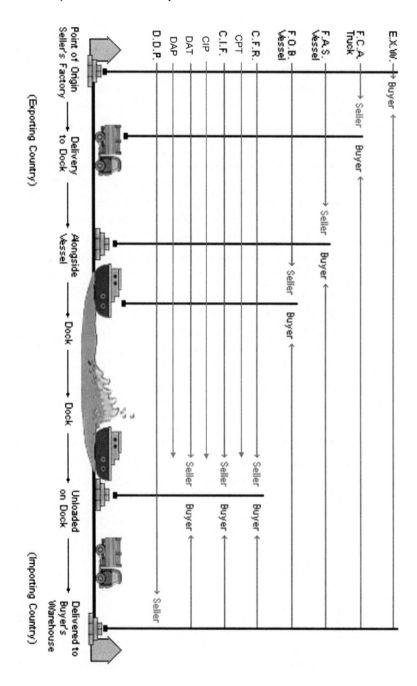

Incoterms and the transfer of risk

Having identified, analysed, and wherever possible explained how Incoterms assist in reducing the risks to which an organisation is exposed in the contract of sale, it is therefore necessary for an individual to decide whether to retain the risk or endeavour to transfer it to the other party. The most common form of risk transfer is by means of insurance which changes an uncertain exposure to a certain cost, i.e. premium that can be budgeted for. In normal circumstances insurance premiums include provision for insurers' overheads and profit plus contributions for the catastrophe element. When dealing with Incoterms, every individual, company or government department is exposed to a wide range of risks. It is inevitable, by nature of probability that financial loss will occur sooner or later. The degree of severity will vary according to circumstances but that some form of loss will occur is beyond doubt.

A prudent contract manager recognising this beyond fundamental truth, will identify practical ways of measuring his own particular exposure, and the only way to identify this is by understanding the risks associated with the Incoterms that you chose during the contract negotiations. That particular Incoterm that you select for that particular situation should be able to assist you in minimising the risk exposure for your company and in the most cost effective manner available. In order, to relate the issue of risk transfer in as far as Incoterms are concerned the writer will examine and highlight where and when the transfer of risks pass from one seller to the buyer

Incoterms and the transfer of risk

Incoterm	Transfer of risk
EXW	When the goods are at the disposal of the buyer
FCA	When the goods have been delivered to the carrier at the named place
FAS	When the goods have been placed alongside the ship
FOB	When the goods pass the ship's rail, at the port of export (origin)
CFR	When the goods pass the ship's rail, at the port of export (origin)
CIF	When the goods pass the ship's rail, at the port of export (origin)
CIP	When the goods have been delivered to the main carrier, at the port of export (origin)
CPT	When the goods have been delivered to the main carrier, at the port of export (origin)
DAT	When the goods once unloaded from the arrival means of transport and are placed at the disposal of the buyer at a named port or place of destination
DAP	When the goods are placed at the disposal of the buyer on the arriving means of transport and ready for unloading at the named place of destination
DDP	When the goods are placed at the disposal of the buyer having been cleared for import and ready for unloading at the named place of destination.

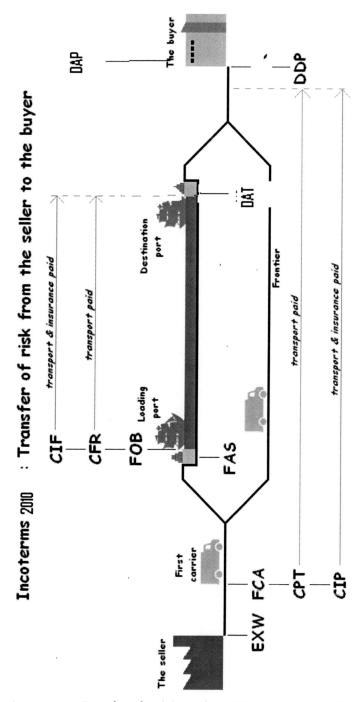

Incoterms—Transfer of Risk by Robert Wielgorski—modified
by Brian Chikwava to include new terms DAT and DAP

Incoterms: checklist of who pays for what

Incoterms® 2010 →	FAS	FOB	CFR	CIF
Services	Payee	Payee	Payee	Payee
Export Packing	S	S	S	S
Marking & Labelling	S	S	S	S
Block and Brace	1	1	1	1
Export Clearance (Licence, EEI/AES)	S	S	S	S
Freight Forwarder Documentation Fees	B	B	S	S
Inland Freight to Main Carrier	S	S	S	S
Origin Terminal Charges	B	S	S	S
Vessel Loading Charges	B	S	S	S
Ocean Freight/Air Freight	B	B	S	S
Nominate Export Forwarder	B	B	S	S
Marine Insurance	3	3	3	S
Unload Main Carrier Charges	B	B	4	4
Destination Terminal Charges	B	B	4	4
Nominate On-Carrier	B	B	B	B
Security Information Requirements	B	B	B	B
Customs Broker Clearance Fees	B	B	B	B
Duty, Customs Fees, Taxes	B	B	B	B
Delivery to Buyer Destination	B	B	B	B
Delivering Carrier Unloading	B	B	B	B

(Note: S = Shipper; B - Buyer

Rules for any mode or modes of transport
EXW = EX WORKS
FCA = FREE CARRIER
CPT = CARRIAGE PAID TO
CIP = CARRIAGE AND INSURANCE PAID TO
DAT = DELIVERED AT TERMINAL
DAP = DELIVERED AT PLACE
DDP = DELIVERED DUTY PAID

Rules for sea and inland waterway transport
FAS = FREE ALONGSIDE SHIP
FOB = FREE ON BOARD
CFR = COST AND FREIGHT
CIF = COST, INSURANCE AND FREIGHT

Incoterms® 2010 →	EXW	FCA	CPT	CIP	DAT	DAP	DDP
Services	Payee	Payee	Payee	Payee	Payee	Payee	Payee
Export Packing	S	S	S	S	S	S	S
Marking & Labelling	S	S	S	S	S	S	S
Block and Brace	1	1	1	1	1	1	1
Export Clearance (License, EEI/AES)	B	S	S	S	S	S	S
Freight Forwarder Documentation Fees	B	B	S	S	S	S	S
Inland Freight to Main Carrier	B	2	S	S	S	S	S
Origin Terminal Charges	B	B	S	S	S	S	S
Vessel Loading Charges	B	B	S	S	S	S	S
Ocean Freight/Air Freight	B	B	S	S	S	S	S
Nominate Export Forwarder	B	B	S	S	S	S	S
Marine Insurance	3	3	3	3	3	3	3
Unload Main Carrier Charges	B	B	4	4	4	S	S
Destination Terminal Charges	B	B	4	4	4	B	S
Nominate On-Carrier	B	B	5	5	5	5	5
Security Information Requirements	B	B	B	B	B	B	B
Customs Broker Clearance Fees	B	B	B	B	B	B	S
Duty, Customs Fees, Taxes	B	B	B	B	B	B	S
Delivery to Buyer Destination	B	B	5	5	5	5	S
Delivering Carrier Unloading	B	B	B	B	B	B	S

Notes: (S = Shipper; B = Buyer) This table is for reference only and is not intended as legal advice.

1. The Incoterms do not allocate this task to Buyer or Seller – to be addressed in the sales contract.

2. FCA Seller's Facility – Buyer pays inland freight; other FCA qualifiers. Seller arranges and loads pre-carriage carrier and pays inland freight to the 'F' delivery place.

3. Marine Insurance – The obligation to arrange insurance is only covered under CIP & CIF. Under all other terms it must be addressed in the sales contract.

4. Terminal Charges paid by Buyer or Seller depends on Carrier practice to include/exclude transport charges.

5. Delivery to Buyer Destination paid by Seller if through Bill of Lading or door-to-door rate to Buyer's destination.

INCOTERMS® 2010	FAS	FOB	CFR	CIF
SERVICES	Who Pays	Who Pays	Who Pays	Who Pays
Export Packing	Shipper	Shipper	Shipper	Shipper
Marking & Labeling	Shipper	Shipper	Shipper	Shipper
Block and Brace	1	1	1	1
Export Clearance (License, EEI/AES)	Shipper	Shipper	Shipper	Shipper
Freight Forwarder Documentation Fees	Buyer	Buyer	Shipper	Shipper
Inland Freight to Main Carrier	Shipper	Shipper	Shipper	Shipper
Origin Terminal Charges	Buyer	Shipper	Shipper	Shipper
Vessel Loading Charges	Buyer	Shipper	Shipper	Shipper
Ocean Freight / Air Freight	Buyer	Buyer	Shipper	Shipper
Nominate Export Forwarder	Buyer	Buyer	Shipper	Shipper
Marine Insurance	3	3	3	Shipper
Unload Main Carrier Charges	Buyer	Buyer	4	4
Destination Terminal Charges	Buyer	Buyer	4	4
Nominate On-Carrier	Buyer	Buyer	Buyer	Buyer
Security Information Requirements	Buyer	Buyer	Buyer	Buyer
Customs Broker Clearance Fees	Buyer	Buyer	Buyer	Buyer
Duty, Customs Fees, Taxes	Buyer	Buyer	Buyer	Buyer
Delivery to Buyer Destination	Buyer	Buyer	Buyer	Buyer
Delivering Carrier Unloading	Buyer	Buyer	Buyer	Buyer

RULES FOR ANY MODE OR MODES OF TRANSPORT

EXW = EX WORKS
FCA = FREE CARRIER
CPT = CARRIAGE PAID TO
CIP = CARRIAGE AND INSURANCE PAID TO
DAT = DELIVERED AT TERMINAL
DAP = DELIVERED AT PLACE
DDP = DELIVERED DUTY PAID

RULES FOR SEA AND INLAND WATERWAY TRANSPORT

FAS = FREE ALONGSIDE SHIP
FOB = FREE ON BOARD
CFR = COST AND FREIGHT
CIF = COST, INSURANCE AND FREIGHT

When is delivery to the carrier completed for all modes of transport?

1. Rail

In the case of rail transport when the goods constitute a wagon load (or a container load carried by rail) the seller has to load the wagon or container in the appropriate manner. Delivery therefore is completed when the loaded wagon or container is taken over by the railway or by another person acting on its behalf.

2. Road

In the case of road transport when loading takes place at the seller's premises, delivery is completed when the goods have been loaded on the vehicle provided by the buyer (EX-Works). When the goods are delivered to a carrier's premises, delivery is completed when they have been handed over to the road carrier or to another person acting on this behalf (FCA).

3. Inland Waterway

In the case of transport by inland waterway, when loading takes place at the seller's premises, delivery is completed when the goods have been loaded on the carrying vessel provided by the buyer (FOB). When the goods are delivered to the carrier's premises, Delivery is completed when they have been handed over to the inland waterway carrier or to another person acting on this behalf.

4. Sea Transport

In the case of sea transport, when the goods constitute a full container load (FCL), delivery is completed when the loaded container is taken over by the sea carrier (CFR and CIF). International traders are encouraged not to not use FOB for containerised shipments, instead use FCA. When the container has been carried to an operator of a transport terminal acting on behalf of the carrier, the goods shall be deemed to have been taken over when the container has entered into the premises of that terminal. In the case of project cargo under FAS delivery is completed when the goods have been placed alongside the ship ready to be loaded on the ship.

5. Air transport

In the case of air transport, delivery is completed when the goods have been handed over to the air carrier or to another company acting on its behalf (CPT or CIP).

Contracts and the use of the Incoterms 2010 rules

It is critically important during the tendering process, depending on the type of sourcing, whether strategic, tactical or project, that the terms of sales be discussed upfront and at every stage of the contract-formulation process.

More importantly, all stakeholders should be aware of both the advantages and the disadvantages of each Incoterm in order to be able make appropriate decisions when dealing with international trade transactions. They are also urged to modernise their operations and adapt to new management techniques and procedures in order to remain competitive in the global market.

The following have to be noted before concluding and signing a contract (this is a requirement introduced by the Incoterms 2010 rules):

1. **Specify your place of departure or port as precisely as possible:**
   If both parties agree on the use of a certain port or named place of departure, it is very important to name it as precisely as possible. This will avoid potential disputes as a result of ambiguity regarding the place. This lack of specifying a place was probably one of the reasons why the experts responsible for the revision decided to incorporate this important point.

   For example, if both parties agree on FCA Incoterms, it would be advisable to state the arrangement as:

   > *'FCA Block H Midrand Industrial park, Midrand Avenue, Midrand, Gauteng, South Africa as per Incoterms® 2010.'*

   This is very specific and the seller will have a clear understanding that he or she will fulfil his or her obligation only once delivery has taken place to the stated address.

2. **The specific Incoterm should be incorporated in the contract of sale:**
   Incoterms apply only if incorporated in the contract of sale or if they are, for example, mentioned in the offer, the sales conditions, the purchase order, the confirmation of an order or if they are stipulated by the parties in separate agreement. With the new revised set of Incoterms and their requirements, it is important to note that whenever you want the Incoterms to apply to your contract, legal members who participate as a cross-functional team must make sure that they should make it clear in their contract through such words as:

   > *'The chosen Incoterms rule including named place or port followed by Incoterms® 2010'.*

In addition to this, it must be stressed that when the parties intend to incorporate Incoterms into their contracts of sale, they should always make an expressed reference to the current version of these terms.

3. **Appropriate Incoterms must be chosen:**
Whenever Incoterms are chosen, it has to be stressed that they must be appropriate to the goods (type, weight, dimensions) that are going to be imported or delivered. In addition, the means of transport (road, rail, air or sea) also plays an influential role in the selection of the appropriate terms of sale. Certain types of goods cannot be delivered by air because of their excessive weight.

However, whichever Incoterm will have been chosen or agreed upon, both parties should always be aware that the interpretation of their contract may well be influenced by customs at a particular port or place being used. It must be emphasised that all the personnel in a company responsible for concluding the contracts must be well trained and have a full understanding of the different Incoterms and their implications, because choosing the wrong or an inappropriate Incoterm for a specific situation may be very costly.

4. **Be aware that Incoterms rules do not give a complete contract of sale:**
As discussed previously (when the issue of misconceptions about Incoterms was highlighted on page 15 above), it is important to ensure that other contractual obligations are incorporated separately, for example payment terms, transfer of ownership of goods and also the consequences of a breach of contract that are normally dealt with in a service-level agreement (SLA). If parties make the assumption that all other contractual aspects are covered by a chosen Incoterm, it will have seriously negative repercussions.

Over the past decade, the court's workload has considerably expanded and many of the cases received have been as a result of the trading community not understanding the importance of creating a contract of sale that looks after the interest of both the seller and the buyer in every international trade deal. Additionally, the misuse of the Incoterms® 2010 Rules could result in huge financial losses for both parties—the seller and the buyer.

Case study

An international mining conglomerate lost several million US dollars, when selling platinum to a Japanese bank in Tokyo, Japan.

The contract of sale stated: 'CFR Zurich, Switzerland' as per Incoterms 2000, whereas the transport contract stated: 'Tokyo, Japan'.

When the contract of sale was drawn up, the accountant, thinking incorrectly that Incoterms related to ownership and had nothing to do with the logistics or movement of goods from the seller to that of the buyer, quoted the wrong Incoterm and stated 'CFR Zurich, Switzerland', because the funds were being transferred from Switzerland. The movement of goods was, however, to Tokyo, Japan.

On arrival in Tokyo, Japan, the platinum cargo was stolen. The mining company instructed the buyer to claim against their insurance policy as it was not the fundamental obligation of the seller to procure insurance when selling CFR. When the buyer endeavoured to claim against his policy, the insurance company stated that the seller was still responsible for the goods as the seller had not filled their fundamental obligation in accordance with the contract of sale, in that the platinum had not been delivered to Zurich, Switzerland.

The buyer was exonerated of any wrong doing and the risk was placed in the hands of the seller. As a result of using the Incoterms incorrectly, the seller lost US$32 000 000.

Factors influencing the choice of Incoterms in contracts

The issues explained below must be taken into account when concluding a contract that has involved buying and selling internationally.

Whenever a contract manager is involved in the negotiation of the contract that requires choosing the applicable Incoterms for that particular situation, he or she should understand that a contract is an agreement in law between persons within which the promise to do something, and not to do something, or deliver something is agreed. Moreover, the fact that people enter into a contract is because they wish to have protection under the law should a dispute arise. In this case both parties have legal recourse. In theory a contract is based on a union of wills or meeting of the minds (*consensus ad idem*); in practice it is difficult to know when people really have agreed. A contract is therefore lawful agreement made by two or more persons within the limits of their contractual capacity with serious intention of creating a legal obligation. A valid contract must contain the following elements:

- The agreement must be lawful.
- Contracting parties must have the capacity to contract.
- The parties must seriously intend that the agreement results in terms that can be enforced.
- The agreement must be communicated by each party to the other by offer and acceptance.
- The terms of the agreement must not be vague.
- There must be reality of consent between the parties.
- The contract must be performable.

Having said this, as long as the intention of both parties is communicated clearly then the contract is a binding agreement. For sales contract to be valid it must create a personal right in the buyer to enforce delivery by the seller. It is therefore advisable that the following be taken into consideration when choosing the appropriate Incoterm to be Included in the sales contract:

1 **Type of cargo**

   The type of cargo being transported plays an important role in the determination of which Incoterm to use. Bulk products conveyed by sea will normally be governed by FAS . . ., FOB . . ., CFR . . . and CIF, all of which facilitate carriage under a charter party arrangement. Break-bulk products conveyed by sea will be governed by FOB . . ., CFR . . . and CIF . . . . Containerised products from an inland source will be governed by the FCA . . ., CPT . . . and CIP . . ., rather than the corresponding FOB . . ., CFR . . . and CIF . . ., because the transfer of risk under the former terms favours containerised cargo, and the terms are ideal where a through rate is provided for transportation. EXW . . ., DAT, DAP . . . and DDP . . . could, of course, be used for any kind of cargo.

2 **Volumes of delivery**

   It is logical to suppose that bigger volumes increase the value of the delivery. FOB is usually used for bigger volumes (greater values) while CFR for smaller volumes (lower values) of the materials. In these situations the importers prefer to take more control over deliveries of greater value and thus they take the responsibility for transportation. In the cases when smaller volumes of are to be delivered, the value of the consignment is lower and importers have less control over transportation which is usually arranged by the supplier.

3 **Risks involved**

   In some cases, the intention to have a greater degree of control over the delivery leads the importers to use EXW when the responsibility and risks for the exporter are minimal, though rarely, and more often FOB is used in the seafood trade. The supplier condition plays an important role in the choice of terms of delivery, thus CIF is usually stipulated by the supplier.

4   Relationship with insurance companies

The relationship with the insurance agencies plays an important role. This means that, if the importers have a good relationship with the insurance company, they may obtain better insurance conditions. In this case the importers prefer to use the terms CFR, FOB or EXW.

5   Calculation of the customs clearance fees

Most companies—mainly in the Russian market—underlined the calculation of customs clearance fees as one of the most important factors for the choice of Incoterm that is why the term 'CIF' is not popular with the Russian importers. In the case of consignment, they usually have a one-year insurance agreement in place. This means that in a case of the term 'CIF' being used, the Norwegian exporter exporting to Russia has to take out extra insurance for a specific consignment. The Russian importer in its turn has to include the price for fish (for example), the price for transportation and insurance in order to calculate customs fee. This makes the customs fee more costly. In order to reduce the customs clearance fee, the respondents prefer to use the terms 'CFR', 'FOB', 'FCA' or 'EXW'.

6   Legislation obstacles and conditions of trade

In some instances, local government policy and regulations may render certain Incoterms unsuitable as one may have obligations over which one has no control and therefore one should avoid using the specific Incoterm. Governments may specify that particular Incoterms be used because, either they wish to promote the transportation of goods by national carriers, or they wish to promote their own domestic insurance market or they may be attempting to save foreign currency. In other parts of the world some conditions under which one is trading could affect the degree of involvement in specific parts of the transport chain. Good examples that can be cited are: port congestion/strikes or other factors which affect the discharging and delivery of the cargo. In addition, there may be no representative available at the destination to resolve the above problems, if they occur.

7 Common practices

In some parts of the world it is common practice that one will find there is serious resistance to the use of certain Incoterms. This is due mainly to the fact that the seller or buyer prefers to keep control of the transport arrangement. A good example would be the Far East market. They prefer to work with the 'C' or 'D' terms of the Incoterms. Furthermore, the supplier condition plays an important role in the choice of terms of delivery, thus CIF is usually stipulated by the supplier. Therefore the use of Incoterms is a common practice in the company that has been formed based on the experience of trade with another specific country.

8 Relations with the carrier

In most cases—sometimes for the importing company—it is cheaper to receive the goods at the exporter's store and to conduct an agreement with the carrier on terms of FOB.

Carriers often give better conditions to their best clients, and therefore some South African importers, for example, obtain better prices for transportation from certain carriers Thus the relationships with the carrier can be mentioned as one of the factors that influences which Incoterm to be used. Some large companies in have in fact signed long-term contracts with carriers and have negotiated fixed rates for a certain period.

In the course of this author's training sessions, a delegate acknowledged that his company chose to use the term 'CIF' because they and their overseas suppliers had better agreements with carriers.

What you need to know and understand about the new features of Incoterms 2010

1. Incoterms 2010 can now be used for domestic trade

At the consultative session regarding the revision of the set of Incoterms 2000 a question was raised regarding what to use for domestic trade. The experts who were responsible for and involved in the drafting of the new set of terms within the Incoterms took this into consideration and decided to officially recognise the new set of Incoterms 2010 to be used and to make them applicable to domestic trade This was a relief to most contracts managers who were responsible for concluding domestic/local contracts.

As mentioned earlier, Incoterms are recognised internationally and by legal authorities. The present writer, while conducting training in the new terms, however, discovered that some large companies had resorted to the use of unrecognised terms that they had developed themselves. A notable example is one large, reputable company that had resorted to using what they called Delivered Cost Included (DCI) and Delivered Cost Excluded (DEC) as their terms of sale for domestic trade. The danger that lies in the use of these unrecognised terms is that that if a dispute arises on the basis of the use of the terms, neither of the parties will have recourse to arbitration.

In various areas of the world, trade blocs, specifically those such as the European Union (EU), have made border formalities between different countries less significant. As a result of this, the perception associated with Incoterms that all Incoterms are traditionally used solely for International sales contracts have now been superseded by this promulgation that Incoterms 2010 can been used for domestic trade and not only when goods pass across national borders, as has traditionally been the case.

There are three possible reasons or developments that prompted or persuaded the ICC to recognise Incoterms 2010 as a set of rules that can be used for domestic trade:

(a) There is a greater willingness on the part of the United States and other developed countries to use Incoterms rules in domestic trade rather than the former Uniform Commercial Code Shipment and Delivery Terms.
(b) Traders across most developed and developing countries commonly use Incoterms rules for purely domestic sale contracts.
(c) There was no internationally recognised set of rules for use for domestic trade.

For these reasons, the new set of Revised Incoterms 2010 may be used officially for domestic trade.

2. Introduction of two new rules in Incoterms 2010

Delivered at Terminal (DAT) and Delivered at Place (DAP) have been introduced literally to replace the four scrapped Incoterms: DAF, DES, DEQ and DDU. This has obviously reduced the number of Incoterms from 13 (Incoterms 2000) to 11 (Incoterms 2010).

Both fall within the category of use, irrespective of mode of transport. In the present author's opinion, these two new rules mean the Incoterms 2000 version DES and DEQ are superimposed, because DAT can be safely used where the Incoterm DEQ was being used—under DAT the named terminal may well be in a port.

As with the replacement of DES with DAP, the arriving 'vehicle' under DAP may well be a ship and the named place of destination may well be a port. As a result, without any major issues, DAP can be used where the Incoterms 2000 DES rule was once used.

3. Information related to customs clearance—'Literature'

Since the 11 September 2001 bombing in the United States and increasing security-related cases involving international trade, there has been a heightened concern from all traders nowadays about security around the movement of goods, requiring verification that goods do not pose a threat to life or property for reasons other than their inherent nature. In this regard the new set of Incoterms 2010 has apportioned responsibilities between the buyer and seller to obtain or to assist in obtaining security-related clearances, such as chain-of-custody information, generally known as 'Literature' in international trade.

The following case study may provide an insight into this:

Case study

A seller sells goods DAT New York, Terminal, USA. The US authorities insist that the buyer provides them with information regarding the contents of the containers within which the goods are stuffed before the vessel on which the containers are carried is allowed into New York. What are the seller's obligations towards the buyer in this regard?

It is therefore important to refer to clause A10 of the Incoterms 2010 booklet. In this case, the seller must assist in supplying the relevant information provided the buyer has requested this information in good time.

4. String sales

As opposed to the sale of manufactured goods as commodities, cargo is frequently sold several times while in transit, 'down a string of sellers and buyers'. If and when this happens, a seller in the middle of the string of transactions does not 'Ship' the goods because these have already been shipped by the first seller in the string. Under this scenario, according to the ICC Incoterms 2010, the seller in the middle of the string therefore performs his obligations towards his buyer not by shipping the goods but by procuring the goods that have been shipped.

5. Variants on Incoterms rules

It is common practice that sometimes both parties want to vary an Incoterm rule later to suit whatever they regard as best in their particular contract of sale. The new rules have introduced a provision that does not prohibit such an alteration. Whatever alteration the parties agree to, however, it is important to note that there are inherent potential dangers and legal implications associated with such an alteration. It is also similar to bending the rules to suit your situation, because, whatever happens after the alteration, the Disputes Board (DB) will always refer to the original rule during arbitration. In order to avoid unnecessary or unwelcome surprises, it is therefore advisable that both parties who need to make the alterations be extremely clear in the contracts and that they use the services of legal advisors when making any alterations. The parties should also make it clear whether they intend to vary the point at which the risk passes from seller to the buyer. Whatever the case may be, the bottom line is that many issues in Incoterms can be modified if there is a conflict between Incoterms and local legal regulations. What matters is whether the both parties can clearly indicate the agreed-upon modification in their contract.

Some words used in Incoterms and their real meaning

In normal circumstances, the words used in Incoterms 2010 rules are supposed to be self-explanatory and not require interpretation. However, questions have been raised and some words have been misinterpreted by readers in a number of cases. Therefore it would be worthwhile to highlight or offer guidance as to the real sense or meaning according to which selected terms are used.

'Delivery'

The word 'delivery' has multiple meanings in trade law and practice, however, in the Incoterms 2010 rules it is used to indicate where the risk for the consequences of loss or damage to the goods passes/ transfers from the seller to the buyer under a specific sales contract. In this regard both notions—delivery and risk—are very important, since the physical delivery and transfer of risk mark the point at which the seller performs what is usually its most significant obligation under the contract of sale, that is, to pass the goods to the buyer.

After a closer examination of both 'delivery' and transfer of risk, it can be concluded that under the applicable law these can be defined differently. It may often be complicated to determine under a particular sales contract when exactly the seller performs his delivery obligation and when risk passes to the buyer. As it is, this may cause a lot of confusion and misunderstandings that might lead to serious conflicts between parties to a contract of sale.

Delivery can take place at the seller's premises, at the buyer's premises or at a point in between. A good example is article 31 of CISG, which fixes delivery at the place where goods are handed over to the first carrier. As indicated in the last section, it makes sense therefore that by incorporating one of the Incoterms rules into a sales contract, both parties can easily clarify precisely where the seller performs his obligation to deliver under a sales contract.

Furthermore, it should be noted that under most Incoterms rules contractual delivery takes place when goods are handed over not directly to the buyer but to a third party—often a carrier—at a predetermined place. In addition, customs for handing over goods to carriers may vary depending on the place. The clear identification of that place and a clear statement of it in contracts therefore avoid the confusion that could arise because different applicable laws might fix the passage of risk at diverging places.

In conclusion to the explanation of the word 'delivery' in use in relation to Incoterms, the Incoterms 2010 rules—as do all prior versions, including the Incoterms 2000 version—respond to the practical need for a clear definition of the contractual place of delivery.

'Carrier'

The term 'carrier' has also been used interchangeably, which has caused some confusion as to what it refers to. However, in the author's view, for the definition of carrier you simply need to refer to the official publication: for the purposes of the Incoterms 2010 rules, the carrier is the party with whom carriage is contracted.[2]

Therefore, who the carrier is will depend on the particular circumstances. For example, with FCA it is likely to be the buyer's forwarder; with CPT, CIP and the D rules it is likely to be the seller's forwarder. With FOB, CFR and CIF it is likely to be the owner of the vessel as determined by the charter party.

---

[2]   ICC Incoterms®2010 page 5.

It is important, therefore, to note that forwarders do indeed have a role as carriers. The best solution is to see who signed the transport document. If it is a forwarder, then they are the carrier; if it is an airline's International Air Transport Association (IATA) air waybill, then it is the airline; if it is a bulk charter B/L, then it is the master of the vessel (on behalf of the vessel owner, as indicated in the C/P); if it is CMR, then it is the trucking company; if it is a CIM, it is the railway company, and so on. Ownership of the actual means of transport does not come into it. Indeed, many shipping lines do not actually own the vessels even with their name sounding as they do: they time charter them from the owner.

'Terminal'

Most people will refer to a port when they hear the word terminal; however, it must be stressed that in the use of the new Incoterms rules the word 'terminal' is described as or refers to 'any place, whether covered or not, such as a quay, warehouse, container yard, rail road or air cargo terminal'.

Goods and services and Incoterms

It is important to note that the application of the rules is confined to the delivery of movable, tangible goods. The Incoterms rules are valid only if they have been agreed upon in explicitly contractual terms, and have been named in purchase agreements, offers/quotations, general purchase and sale conditions, orders, order confirmations, etc, or included in a separate agreement. However, a debate was raised during the forum held in Johannesburg in August 2010 regarding the use of Incoterms when importing or exporting electricity,the writer wishes to share the views raised during the deliberations.

Electricity energy trade contract and the use of Incoterms® 2010

The introduction to the Incoterms 2010 book refers to sales of 'goods'.[3] without any further definition of this word in the book. One would suggest that the best understanding of 'goods' in relation to Incoterms is that they are an item or items which are capable of being stopped for an indeterminate period of time at a customs border and detained for examination.

With this notion, therefore, I believe electricity would be in the same category as software transmitted electronically, where Incoterms do not apply. Under the HS 2716 heading, several countries have regulated the international trade in electricity as energy. Controls and specific customs procedures have been designed to deal with its particularities. For example, for practical reasons, customs clearance is done after the

---

[3]   ICC Incoterms 2010 page 1.

entry of the goods into the territory and according to measurements at the power plant. Electricity energy is thus considered to qualify as a good and by that it is subject to the rules of the World Trade Organisation (WTO).[4]

On the other hand, electricity must be able to be classified in the International Convention on the Harmonized Commodity Description and Coding System (HS Nomenclature) as it is certainly a commodity; but what that classification would be is still a mammoth task to explain. Neither do the Incoterms experts have the capabilities to classify it.

As far as Incoterms are concerned, one would suspect there is a term available that could be amended, by agreement, to take into account the fact that there is not a carrier, etc., in the normal sense of Incoterms.

Several people have tried to address pipeline transactions in the revision but were unable to do so for the following reasons:

1. Frequently, the product shipped is not the product actually received. Instead, a specified product is placed into the pipeline at the seller's end, and a fungible product (ie one that precisely or acceptably replaces another) is withdrawn at the buyer's end.
2. There are already numerous trade practices to address this situation.

In the case of electricity energy and similar 'goods' or 'products', the phrase 'virtual delivery' says it all.

Importing or exporting electricity applies to a greater or lesser extent to fluids, or natural gas.

Readers are encouraged to read or refer to the link to WTO, which covers some of what has been highlighted earlier.[5]

---

[4] Source: Leonardo Macedo[(1)] Electricity energy and the WTO customs valuation agreement.

[5] <http://www.wto.org/english/res_e/publications_e/wtr10_forum_e/wtr10_2july10_e.htm>

Overall, this tends to support the assertion that electricity is a 'good' for the purposes of customs and trade and as such there is a 'delivery, transportation, risk, etc and whereas Incoterms obviously do not wish to become involved in these types of 'delivery', I reiterate my opinion that an amended Incoterm could well suffice to address this. If, surely, electricity is to be considered as 'goods', then Incoterms could and should apply, and there must surely be a way for people who produce electricity to know how to measure which quantity of electricity is sent through the cables and can be invoiced to the buyer.

Principal errors made by importers and/or exporters in the use of Incoterms in contracts

Despite the fact that Incoterms were developed to simplify international transactions and to make their application in international trade more precise, there are still a number of reasons why they often fail to achieve their intended purpose. In most cases, it is due to lack of knowledge of the terms as well as inaccuracy and even too little effort put in when utilising or applying them. During this author's working career in the international trade and logistics industry, the following have been identified as the problems most frequently associated with use of Incoterms:

1. Most people use **a sea-freight term** such as **FOB** or **CIF** when consigning goods **by air or road freight.**
2. **Incoterms are not quoted at all in the contracts.** This makes it very difficult to apportion responsibilities to either the buyer or seller and even to manage and/or monitor these contracts
3. **Doing more under the term than required**, for example, loading under 'Ex-Works'.
4. **Out-dated Incoterms being used.** Many people are not aware that a new version of the Incoterms was issued in January 2010 and that some original Incoterms—such as DDU, DES DAF and DEQ—are no longer in use. Many, however, still continue making use of them. Worse still, one may find that an Incoterm is quoted followed by 2000 instead of year 2010 or no year at all. Although, in a few cases, this may not mean much difference when considering the obligations, but in certain

cases, for example FCA, there are very significant differences and the use of the wrong edition can be critical.

5. **Incorrect abbreviation of the Incoterm are being quoted**. One will occasionally come across situations where the invoice does not indicate the full Incoterm. For example, instead of EXW and while it may still be possible or logical to work out which Incoterm was involved it should be pointed out the seller or buyer that the correct version always has three letters

6. **Not being protected against when things go wrong because the 'term' quoted has never been reviewed against the legal issues**. In practice, some contracts have quoted the unrecognised Incoterms such as Delivered Cost Included (DCI) or Delivery Cost Included (DCE). This is dangerous as these terms are not recognised by legal authorities and therefore using these terms might lead a company having no recourse should a dispute arises out of the use of these unrecognised or illegal terms.

7. **Parties choose the wrong Incoterm for their particular trade.** It is common practice that some people use DDP, when the seller is unable to meet the registration requirements of overseas customs authorities.

8. **Parties fail to reference the Incoterm with sufficient clarity**. The issue of precision where lack of familiarity with the terminology results in terms such as: FOB South African port being quoted or shown. This will result in all the relevant costs covered by the Incoterms rule being included. While this may be due to the parties wanting to cover all eventualities, it is critical for the preparation of the quotation or estimate that the exact port is known when working out the transport costs,

9. **The mode of transport not taken into consideration**. Certain shipments—as most international practitioners have experienced—are more suited to a particular Incoterm, owing to the method/mode of transport used. It is therefore critical, when, if the way in which the cargo is transported changes, then the existing Incoterm should be reviewed for suitability. With the advent of multi-modalism there are certain commodities and cargo that are now being containerised which were previously transported as break-bulk.

10. **Resistant to change—conservatism.** How many people have heard clients state: 'We have been using FOB or DDP for several years ever since we stated this company and we have not experienced problems?' Experience has taught this author that it is not easy to convince clients that they are using an inappropriate or unsuitable Incoterm. However, it is common practice that one should always be prepared for such difficult clients who simply are not prepared to accept change positively simply because no-one else ever questioned or asked—'Why?'

11. **General lack of knowledge about Incoterms**. I have occasionally come across a scenario during my working experience where a client has queried the charges on inaccurate grounds and it could save considerable time if you are able to point this out at the onset and resolve the issue promptly. Generally, most people are not adequately trained to deal with Incoterms, yet they play a crucial role in the formulation of contracts with overseas or external suppliers. It is therefore recommended that everyone dealing with the drafting of contracts of sale must receive proper training that is facilitated by accredited trainers.

Establishing the appropriate Dispute Boards (DBs) when negotiating business contracts

Very often, questions have been raised with regard to how parties resolve their disputes during the contract period, and many contract practitioners have no idea how to go about doing so. Dispute Boards (DBs) are usually set up at the outset of a contract to assist the parties informally, if they so desire, in resolving disagreements arising in the course of the contract and to make recommendations or decisions regarding disagreements by any of the parties. Disagreements can include the misinterpretation of a particular Incoterm by either party.

It is therefore advisable to choose the appropriate DB when negotiating your business contract and it should be specified whether the DB is to be a Dispute Review Board (DRB), a Dispute Adjudication Board (DAB) or a Combined Dispute Board (CDB).

Dispute Review Board (DRB)

The DRB issues 'recommendations' with respect to any dispute referred to it and constitutes a relatively consensual approach to dispute resolution. If no party expresses dissatisfaction with a recommendation within a stated time period, the parties contractually agree to comply with the recommendation. If a party does express dissatisfaction with the recommendation within such time period, that party may refer the dispute to arbitration, if the parties have so agreed, or to the courts. Pending a ruling by the arbitral tribunal or the court, the parties may voluntarily comply with the recommendation but are not bound to do so.

Dispute Adjudication Board (DAB)

The DAB issues 'decisions' with respect to any dispute referred to it and this constitutes a less consensual approach to dispute resolution. By contractual agreement, the parties must comply with a decision without delay as soon as they receive it. If a party expresses dissatisfaction with a decision within a stated time period, it may refer the dispute to arbitration, if the parties have so agreed, or to the courts; but the parties meanwhile remain contractually bound to comply with the decision unless and until the arbitration tribunal or the court rules otherwise. If no party expresses dissatisfaction with a decision within the stated time period, the parties contractually agree to remain bound by it.

Combined Dispute Board (CDB)

The CDB usually issues recommendations with respect to any dispute referred to it but may issue a decision if a party so requests and no other party objects. In the event of an objection, the CDB will decide whether to issue a recommendation or a decision on the basis of the criteria set forth in the rules. The CDB thus offers an intermediate approach between the DRB and the DAB.

The essential difference between a decision and a recommendation is that the parties are required to comply with the former without delay as soon as they receive it, whereas a recommendation must be complied with only if no party expresses dissatisfaction within a stated time limit. If a party is dissatisfied with a DB's determination of a given dispute, whether in the form of a decision or in the form of a recommendation, it may refer the dispute to arbitration, if the parties have so agreed, or to the courts. The DB's determination is admissible in any such further proceedings.

However, it is critical to stress that whenever you are setting up these DBs, the process of establishment must be in accordance with the provisions of the parties' contract or, where the contract is silent, in accordance with the ICC Dispute Board Rules.

Conclusions and recommendations

In an attempt to circumvent this problem of inconsistent and varied interpretation of trade terms in the international trade market, the ICC in 1936 drafted international commercial terms—what is now known as 'Incoterms® 2010'? The ICC mainly drafted these terms with the intention of promoting a universally accepted understanding of international trade terms that would help to avoid misunderstandings. These terms are now commonly used in agreements and contracts to determine such matters as: when the responsibility for transporting the goods switches from the seller to the buyer; who is responsible for insuring the goods, and at what point liability transfers from seller to buyer. Contrary to common belief, Incoterms do not deal with the transfer of title or ownership of goods.

In order to ensure that the Incoterms 2010 terms apply, buyers and sellers should specify 'Incoterms 2010' on all contractual documents. It should also be noted that whenever a trade term is cited on a document, the wording 'Incoterms 2010' should be referred to along with the specific location. For example, the term 'Free on Board' (FOB) should always be accompanied by a reference to the port of shipment. Example of correct usage:

FOB Durban Port under Incoterms 2010 rules.

Because Incoterms are standard, they are used in business contracts to reduce confusion and avoid traders experiencing difficulties in understanding the import requirements and the shipping requirements in other countries. Therefore, using the correct and appropriate Incoterm clarifies the contracts you have with your suppliers or customers and doing so is critical to sustaining contractual business. Although using Incoterms in contracts is not compulsory, they are recognised by all customs posts and courts worldwide, and it is therefore quite critical that you always incorporate them in your sales contracts. It is also important to note that Incoterms are not law and will not resolve all the problems that can occur in trade; but generally one encourages and expects Incoterms 2010 to be well received by the trade.

As with any change, work will be required within trading companies to ensure that they are ready for this change and have made the necessary amendments to their standard contracts in future. And encourage their employees who use international commercial terms to receive training from accredited trainers If this work is not done, this is a potential recipe for disputes.

Questions about case studies of Incoterms

Note: These case studies should be used in conjunction with the *International Chamber of Commerce (ICC) Incoterms® 2010* book.

1. **EXW—Ex Works:**

   a. EXW—Must seller load on buyer's collecting vehicle?

   b. EXW—What happens if seller assists with the loading anyway?

   c. Customs and Excise in South Africa requires the seller to provide proof of export when selling on EXW basis. What impact would this have on the seller's and buyer's duties under the Incoterm®2010 rules?

   d. In a contract between a South African manufacturer based in Midrand Gauteng, South Africa and a South African Distributor (the contract is described as 'EX-Works Sebenza—BKC Warehouse as per Incoterms® 2010 rules', and promising the arrival of the goods in Sebenza) the goods are lost or damaged en-route from the exporters premises to Sebenza, who bears the risks of that loss or damage?

2. **FCA—Free Carrier:**

   a. FCA—Who bears the cost and risk of loading the goods at origin and unloading at the destination?

b. FCA—Who pays: (1) Terminal handling charges at port of loading? (2) Export clearance? (3) Transport cost up to the FCA delivery point (named place) or up to the main carrier's receipt of the goods? and(4) airport charges and transport security fee?

c. FCA—Is seller obligated to stow the goods in buyer's container upon delivery on seller's location?

d. The carrier engaged by the buyer has been charged by port authorities in Cape Town, which is the port named as the place of delivery in a contract of sale, concluded under FCA, Cape Town as per the Incoterms 2010 rules. The carrier refuses to lift the goods unless the seller pays the carrier for such charges. The seller now invoices the buyer for the same charges. Must the buyer pay the seller for such charges?

3   **FOB—FREE ON BOARD:**

a. In what circumstances would you recommend using FOB rather FCA? And in what circumstances FAS rather than FOB?

b. In a sales contract, on FOB as per the Incoterms rules 2010, when is ownership in the goods transferred to the buyer?

c. Goods sold on FOB terms are destroyed by a fire in a warehouse in the port of loading. Must the buyer pay the price?

d. Who pays Terminal Handling Charges (THC) in the country of export?

e. What is the ship's rail and what is its significance?

f. Who pays for pre-carriage?

g. Must seller make sure that the goods are stowed/ trimmed on board the ship?

4 CIP—Carriage Insurance Paid:

a. If the seller sells goods CIP Tripoli, as per the Incoterms 2010 rules, will the seller's invoice include the carriage of the goods to Tripoli or only the insurance costs?

b. If a sales contract provide for CIP Heathrow Airport, London, and clearly stating the address at at designated freight forwarder's terminal as per the Incoterms® 2010 rules. The airport authorities charge the freight forwarder for moving of the goods within Heathrow airport, and the freight forwarder now charges the buyer for these movements. Must the buyer pay the freight forwarder, and if he does, can he recover those charges from seller?

c. In question b, above, imagine the goods are damaged within the airport, must the buyer pay the seller the price due under the sales contract?

5 CPT—Carriage Paid To:

a. Where goods are sold on CPT under the Incoterms 2010 rules, are the goods delivered when the seller hands the goods over to the first carrier, or when they successfully reach the agreed destination?

b. In question a, above, who is the first carrier? And from which point must the seller ensure that the goods are insured?

6 DAT—Delivered at Terminal:

a. The seller sells on DAT under the Incoterms 2010 terms rules The goods were carried in containers, It is now a week since the goods were removed by the buyer from the agreed terminal. The buyer discovers today that the goods in two containers were damaged. Can the buyer claim the whole or part of the price back from the seller or can the buyer claim the equivalent in damages?

b. Where goods are being sold by a South African Company to a Zambian buyer, which of the following three Incoterms 2010 rules is appropriate: DAT, DAP or DDP?

c. A seller sells goods DAT New York, Terminal, USA. The US authorities insist that the buyer provides them with information regarding the contents of the containers within which the goods are stuffed before the vessel on which the containers are carried is allowed into New York. What are the sellers' obligations towards the buyer in this regard?

7 DDP—Delivered Duty Paid:

a. A contract of sale is agreed DDP Hong Kong by air. The buyer wants the seller to pay up to the buyer's premises in Hong Kong. Is the buyer entitled to this part of the transport charges? How might any doubt about the matter have been avoided?

8 DAP—Delivered At Place:

a. Can DAT or DAP be used where the terminal or the place is at a seaport?

9 CFR—Cost and Freight:

a. A seller agrees to sell goods CFR Port Elizabeth, as per the Incoterms 2010 rules. The goods were shipped in Singapore, but the goods are actually discharged in Cape Town on the seller's instruction.

Who now bears the cost of transhipping the goods from Cape Town to Port Elizabeth? If the goods are damaged while they are Cape Town, who bears the risk of their loss or damage while the goods.

b. A seller of grain has bought goods already on board a vessel; can he sell goods on the basis of CFR terms rules? And if the goods are covered by an electronic bill of lading, would that cause problems?

10 **CIF—Cost Insurance and Freight**

a. Who pays terminal handling charges (THC) at the port of arrival?

b. If the goods are sold CIF Rotterdam, in Netherlands according to the Incoterms 2010 rules, does it mean that if goods are damaged in transit, the buyer automatically has the right against the insurer for the loss of goods?

Answers to case study questions

1 ExW—Ex-works

a. No, the buyer must load on the collecting vehicle at the buyer's cost and risk.(Ex-works A4)

b. In case of an accident during loading a dispute over liability may arise. If the seller insists on loading onto the collecting vehicle, it should be stated that loading is at the seller's cost and risk" in the contract.

c. It has to be stated in the contract that the buyer will provide proof of export.

d. This risk lies with the South African manufacturer (A4 and A5) because manufacturer has not fulfilled his obligation to deliver to a named place.(A4 and A5)

2 FCA

a. FCA—seller loads the goods at origin and buyer unloads the goods and destination (A4)

b. (1)—buyer, (2)—seller, (3)—seller, (4)—buyer

c. Loading at origin is at the seller's cost and risk. Unloading at destination is at the buyer's cost and risk.

d. Yes—the buyer must pay refer to A6 and A4.

3 FOB—Free on Board

a. Loading cost and type of cargo.

b. When he has paid for it.

c. No, the goods were not on board yet.

d. The seller pays THC in the port of export.

e. A light structure serving as a guard at the outer edge of a ship's deck. Risk transfer point is the 'ship's rail'.

f. Seller pays pre-carriage up to the ship's rail at the port of export.

g. No, stowing/trimming is at the cost and risk of the buyer.

4 CIP—Carriage Insurance Paid

a. Under CIP yes, the seller has to pay both costs (carriage Insurance Paid) (A6): he or she has to pay for both insurance and freight.

b. Yes, he can pay and recover from seller (A4) and A6 because letter has to deliver to the designated freight forwarders terminal.

c. B5, A4 yes (buyer must pay).

5 CPT—Carriage Paid To:

a. (A4) when goods are handed over to First carrier.

b. B4

6 DAT—Delivered at Terminal

a. Buyer cannot claim back since he or she has assumed the risk a week ago (B4)—seller has no obligation of insurance (A5)

b. Could use all of them DDP no duties applicable between South Africa and Zambia.

c. A10 the seller must assist in providing relevant information.

7 DDP—Delivered Duty Paid

a. DDP named place and address should have been stated: that is, DDP named place.

8 DAP—Delivered At Place

Yes—place can be at sea port so you can use both of them. (A4)

9 CFR—Cost Insurance and Freight

a. The seller bears the cost of transhipping from CPT to PE. It is the responsibility of the buyer to pay for the damages at Cape Town. Insurance is covered by buyer throughout the transit.

b. Yes the electronic B/L can be accepted, He can buy of FOB basis

10 CIF—Carriage Insurance Paid To:

a. Buyer pays THC and Port Charges.

b. Yes (CIF).

References and further reading

ICC Dispute Board Rules

ICC Guide to Incoterms® 2010

Incoterms®2010 Rules

E Jolivet, General Counsel, ICC International Court of Arbitration and Deputy Director, ICC Dispute Resolution Services, Paris, September 2011

JR Stock & DM Lambert (2001) *Strategic Logistics Management* 4 ed New York: McGraw Hill

http://www.wto.org/english/res_e/publications_e/wtr10_forum_e/ wtr10_2july10_e.htm

Acronyms (other than Incoterms)

CDB	Combined Dispute Board
CFC	Client Foreign Currency
CIPS	Chartered Institute of Purchasing and Supply
DAB	Dispute Adjudication Board
DB	Dispute Board
DRB	Dispute Review Board
EMLog	European Master Logistician
EU	European Union
IATA	International Air Transport Association
ICM	Institute of Commercial Management
ICC	International Chamber of Commerce
SLA	service-level agreement
THC	Terminal handling charges
WTO	World Trade Organisation

Acknowledgements:

Thank you to the many people in the supply chain management, transport and logistics, and freight forwarding industries who have shared their ideas, answered queries and generally discussed their experiences with me. Thank you also to all delegates who shared their expertise, practical experiences in conferences papers, articles and reports. These have provided examples of good practice throughout the book. A great many thanks must go to all participants who have attended my trainings and workshops at Eskom and whose questions, comments and general experiences have helped me to develop my ideas and understanding of the topic. I would also like to thank Candice Robertson, the designer, for her feedback and help. Finally, thank you to Fadzai for providing me with her constant support during this project.

Lightning Source UK Ltd.
Milton Keynes UK
UKOW03f1848030414

229381UK00001B/36/P